VALUE YOU!

IF YOU VALUE YOURSELF, YOU WON'T DO THE THINGS YOU DO!

Nina Johnson

VALUE YOU!
If You Value Yourself,
You Won't Do The Things You Do!

U.S. Copyright © 2021 No. **1-10142774811**

Published 2021 by Nina Johnson

Unless otherwise noted, all Scripture quotations are taken from the **King James Version** of the Bible.

Printed in the United States of America

ISBN-13: 978-0-578-83461-0

Table of Contents

DEDICATION

I would like to dedicate this book to my children because of them, I became a teacher, trainer, disciplinarian, and most of all, a loving, caring mother to them.

ACKNOWLEDGEMENTS

I would like to thank my LORD and Savior, JESUS CHRIST, for keeping me through everything that I have been through and for birthing this book out of me.

SPECIAL THANKS

I would like to thank my Pastor Blanche Dowdell and her husband Johnny Dowdell for helping me with this book and all the teaching they gave me. I would like to thank Pastor Deardra Johnson for all of the hard work she put into helping make this book a success.

INTRODUCTION

My desire is that females of all ages will understand that they have great value, learn to cherish those values, and begin to develop into beautiful, secure, prosperous, and virtuous women, the women that God says they are to become.

DAUGHTER'S DEDICATION

Strong. Confident. Loving. Caring. Beautiful. Hardworking. Those are just a few words that come to mind when I think about a mother. My mother. From the moment that I can remember, my mother has always been there. Through every bruised knee, hospital visit, late-night bad dreams' you name it, she's been there as a comfort all throughout my life.

There aren't many like her. She raised my sisters and me to love and respect ourselves. She taught us that we can expect anyone to treat us right if we didn't love ourselves. That's right, loving yourself is first. I can remember growing up and having friends whose parents would let them do whatever they wanted to do while I stayed at home. Yep, my parents were old fashioned. I remember hearing her say plenty of times that we were her kids, so she was going to take care of us. Not anyone else. Not the lady across the street or the pastor. Her and my father. We were their responsibility to raise and instill the correct values in. I've always respected them for that. She is the blueprint for living as a mother.

When I was in elementary school and my mother telling my sisters and me about her rape and molestation story, I can remember. I couldn't have been older than 10 at the time. I can't remember the exact words that she said, but I can remember the lesson I learned. That was that you never let anyone define who you are as a woman and to walk with dignity. Also, to wait for someone that will treat me like the queen that I am. Never settle for less than. I felt deep within that I must love myself and carry myself as a young lady with pride. I told you she is one of a kind.

I can guarantee you that as you read this book, your life will be touched. You will cry, be happy, and everything in between. Life has taught my mother many lessons that she is willing to share with you. I Pray that you are blessed by this book and that you. Will take away the same lessons that my mother taught my siblings and me throughout life. I also pray that this book will be healing to your life in areas that may need it. Be blessed.

FORWARD

I had the pleasure of meeting Nina Johnson many years ago when we served in church together. When we met, she was a young, single mother of two small children and pregnant with her third child. Although she did not fit the regular "church" profile, she possessed a desperate desire to seek God and obtain a real, authentic relationship with Him as Father, through Christ Jesus.

I met her during one of the most vulnerable times in her life when she was keenly aware that the people in the church appeared to accept her on the outside while quietly judging her in the inner circles. She was the poster child for the broadly accepted saying, "There ain't no hurt like a church hurt."

Her desire to understand who God was and how He saw her gave her an underlying strength to remain in the "church" atmosphere. Hence, she often caused additional hurt, pain, and rejection of those who didn't meet the outlined religious standard.

I observed her stand in the most delicate situation of being an unwed mother in the church full of judging eyes and opinions that indicated and secretly related that "She should know better by now." Instead of running and giving up, Nina stayed. Nina stood with her hope in the Lord far outweighing anything that anyone else could say about her or do to her.

I believe that her commitment to stand despite her circumstances caused the Father in all His mercy to lovingly connect her with the strongest, most committed. A loving prayer warrior, I have been privileged to serve with Elder Linda Hall.

Elder Hall became an anchor in Nina's life and began erecting a foundational spiritual wall around her that gave her the tools necessary to stand, grow up in the Spirit, grow in prayer and intercession, and grow up strong and capable in the things of the Lord. Even when things were less than perfect, her connection with Elder Hall helped her remain securely connected to the Lord. When Nina experienced situations that would foster rejection or shame, Elder Hall stood with her without demands, without judgment, and without persecution, but rather a simple example of love and commitment that came from living and walking close to the Father.

I often sat on the sidelines watching and cheering as God stayed faithful to His word giving her the tools and the mentorship that caused a delicate flower to blossom into a secure woman of God, a prayer warrior in her own rights.

When Nina's relationship with her biological mother was shaky and heavily strained, God secured her need for a mother by sending her a spiritual mother in "Mama Hall."

What is even more impressive is to be able to witness Nina being able to take what she learned and deposit it into the lives of her daughters. I've watched her grow into well trained, well mannered, humble young ladies, each pursuing a successful future.

As of this date, Nina has one daughter who has successfully graduated from college, another college freshman. Her youngest is a senior in high school on course for graduation.

When her daughters were at a point that they needed additional spiritual covering, Nina thought it not robbery to send her daughters to our ministry to oversee their spiritual maturity. You see, it was not about her needs and desires as a woman of God but a desire to make sure her daughters' spiritual needs were met in a way that would allow them to grow and soar. I can say that I am truly honored to know that she would think enough of God in me to place her daughters under the care of our ministry.

So, Nina Johnson isn't just talking when she speaks of bringing value into the lives of young ladies by any means possible, or the need for mentorship and spiritual oversight; she has implemented the process of love and mentorship that God has given her into the lives of her daughters and any other young lady that would dare to listen and learn.

What you are about to read in this book is not just a story. No, I have had the distinct pleasure of watching Nina walk the walk and not just talk the talk. Her walk is real, Nina is real, her love and commitment to the Lord is real, and her desire to see women of all ages see their true worth is indisputable.

This book is a product of Nina's belief that God can help anyone and will place just the right people in their lives to help them even when times are hard. This is a book full of her experiences. This book was birthed out of her ability to see God plant a small seed within her, nurture it and protect it until it could grow and become strong.

I urge you to read this book and allow it to minister God's love and the great value He sees within you securely into your heart.

To Nina Johnson, my sister, my friend, I say, "I love you, and I am so very proud that you love young women so much that you dared to expose all of your weaknesses to bring others strength. It is a pleasure and an honor to walk this walk with you."

Pastor Deardra L. "Dee" Johnson
Co-Pastor, Greatness Ministries
Orlando, Melbourne/Palm Bay, Florida

When you are feeling bad about yourself, then start saying these Affirmation.

AFFIRMATION

1. I am beautiful
2. I am Intelligent
3. I am not a victim but a victor
4. I am the beloved of GOD
5. I am worthy of love
6. I love myself
7. I am kind
8. I am a good steward over what GOD has blessed me with
9. I am a wealthy woman
10. I am FREE

CHAPTER 1 - LOST VALUES

A mother is always happy and relieved when she has delivered her child. As mothers, we set out to rear our children in the right direction, but sometimes the pressure of life causes us to get off track. The scripture states, "Train up a child in the way they should go and when they get old, they will not depart from it." (Proverbs 22:6) Children are supposed to learn values from their parents, but often we see children learning from their peers. In this chapter, I will share a little of my childhood.

When I was about 5 or 6 years old, I was molested by a family member. He scared me to let him put his penis inside of my vagina by telling me that he would tell my mom that I was in the abandoned house with my male friend playing. I wasn't supposed to be out of the yard. My friend wanted me to play with him, so I went with him to play in the Pecan Archer. We decided that we would go play in the abandoned house, and while we were playing, my uncle came inside and scared us. He told me if I didn't let him touch me, he would tell my mom about me. I was terrified of my mom because she was so mean. I knew if he told my mom that I snuck out the yard that I would get a whooping. Therefore I agreed because I didn't know what he wanted to do, plus my friend said he didn't want to get in trouble. I wished someone had taught me about good touch, bad touch. That day changed my life. He pulled my shorts down and made me lie down while he tried to put his penis in me. Mind you, my friend was right there watching. When he jumped on top of me to put his penis in me, I started screaming, and my friend started running and yelling. I believed that's why he didn't have full intercourse with me. All I remember is it hurt so bad, and I had a hard time walking. I cried all the way home, and guess what he did? My uncle ran off and left me. That night I told my mom that I was hurting in between my legs, and she said, "You probably fell off that bicycle. You will be alright. Now go sit down." Imagine being 5 or 6 years old, and you go to your mother, and she tells you that after you have been violated.

I felt like don't nobody care about me. She never took the time to check my bottom to see why I was hurting. She just assumed that I fell off the bicycle. If she had checked me out or asked me some questions, she would have known something had happened to me.

That day caused me to feel unloved and full of hatred at the same time. I hated my uncle for years because he would catch me somewhere by myself, and he always tried to have sex with me. I learned on my own to run from him because I didn't want to experience that pain again. He was full of all the wrong values, which caused him to cause harm to me and others. This man caused me to not know how valuable I was. What kind of values did he teach? Instead of producing positive values, I produced negative values; low self-esteem, worthlessness, unlovable, and worst of all, how to allow others to violate me.

I grew up with all these emotions down on the inside. I embraced low self-esteem, and I always felt unloved, but thanks be to my God who gives us the victory through Jesus Christ, my Lord. I hated my mom as well because I felt like she didn't care.

I grew up looking for someone to love me. I became promiscuous as a teen because I wanted to be loved, so I would date different boys and find myself allowing them to violate me.

I was 13 years old, and I wanted to go to the teen center. I asked my mother could I go, and she said yes, but I had to be home at 12:00 a.m. I went to the teen center, and I enjoyed being with my friends. While in the place, I kept a watch on the clock to get home on time. I left the teen center, and on the way, home I felt someone was walking behind me, so I said to myself that I would go home where some light was.

I went home through a dirt road that had houses on it and a little light. The person was still walking behind me then he called my name. I turned around, and it was a young guy that I knew from school. He walked with me through the path, talking to me, and then we got into a dark area, and he raped me. He kept trying to hug me, and I said to him, don't do that, and I had to get home. He pushed me down and pulled my shorts down, and he raped me. During that time, I was on my period, and I was late getting home. I cried all the way home, and I thought to myself, this has happened to me again, and I'm tired of men hurting me.

When I got home, my mom was waiting for me. When I walked into the house, she didn't ask me why I was late. She just started beating me with aboard. I hated my mom even more. She wouldn't let me explain to her what happened. She just started beating me. All I could think about is how I wanted to get away from her and the town I was born in.

I went through many heartaches, and I had some hard times because I wanted to be loved. I ended up in an abusive relationship because my daddy wasn't there, and I didn't know how a man was supposed to treat a woman. I saw my mom's boyfriend cheating and beating on her all the time, so I thought that was the way of life.

I left home at the age of 15 with this man who claimed that he loved me. I believed he did love me, but he didn't know how to treat a woman because he wasn't taught. I felt like a piece of property when I was with him. He was very protective of me, but he cheated on me and beat me. I wasn't allowed to go anywhere without him or his family members. I couldn't have friends. I used to pray and ask God to get me out of that situation. After living with him for three years, he went to prison, and I could finally get out of the relationship.

After he went to prison, I started to go to clubs and drinking. I wanted to be a teenager again, but I had 2 children, and I had to be a mother. I paid the daughter of a friend of mine to babysit so that I could party. I went out partying so much because I was trying to forget my past.

One night I was lying on my sofa, and I started remembering what happened to me when I was a little girl and a teenager. The thoughts of all those things caused me to drink heavily.

I met a good man in 1990, but I couldn't be what he needed me to be because I was miserable inside. I caused him a lot of heartaches. I would go through a period of not letting him touch me because I would remember what happened to me, and I felt so nasty. And when he would touch me, I would go back to my little girl stage and start crying because I felt like he was violating me. I went through periods of not having enough sex. I wanted sex all day, every day, and if he didn't have sex with me, I would start an argument with him and accuse him of being with another woman.

God started drawing me to Himself in 1994 after giving birth to three babies from three different men. I was so depressed because I hadn't dealt with all those issues from the molestation, rape, and abuse. A good friend of mine started to go to church, and she would always invite me to go with her. I always told her I'm not ready to go to church because I knew if I went, I would give God my life.

I went to a club one night, and I was driving home very late, and I was sleepy. I drifted off to sleep, and God woke me up just before I hit a light pole. I told the Lord that night that I would be in church the next Sunday morning, and I went. I wasn't ready to let go of myself for God, but He was still calling. Eventually, I surrendered my will to HIM. But even after all that, I was still miserable inside because I hadn't forgiven my uncle, daddy, and mom.

I learned my true worth and could overcome the negative values of my childhood. Jesus had to help me forgive those people who had hurt me. I was messing up so badly sometimes. One day I would be doing well, and the next day I was full of all those negative emotions. I'd tell God all I wanted was to be and feel loved.

I learned that I had to let go of all those negative emotions and allow GOD to show me who I was. It took some years to let it go, but God has ways of ministering to you to let you know who He is and what He can do if we let Him.

GOD's power caused me to forgive everyone who had hurt me, and I tell you to this day; I love them, and I know God allowed all of this for a purpose in my life. If we knew how valuable we were, then we wouldn't do what we do, things that will cause harm us or others.

Parents, especially mothers, teach their children how to love themselves and know that they are valuable. The scripture states, "Train up a child in the way they should go and when they get old, they will not depart from it." That means that we, as parents, are supposed to teach them values. It is not your pastor's job or their school teacher's job to teach them how valuable they are. The pastor and the teachers just come in and reinforce what we have taught them about themselves.

I say to every person that is reading this book that you are important, you are special. No matter what has happened in your life, you are someone who has it going on, so don't let the devil make you think that you are nobody.

Young ladies remember that "you are fearful and wonderfully made by God." (Psalm 139) Ladies, Don't let anyone determine your self-worth. You are more valuable than you can ever think or imagine.

In the next chapter, I will tell you just how valuable that God says that you are.

CHAPTER 2 - DADDY'S GIRL

When my mother and father were together, I was a daddy's girl. I loved my daddy so much. When he and my mother broke up, a part of me was broken too.

I remember my daddy combing my hair and taking me with him almost wherever he would go. He always called me his little princess, and that's exactly how he made me feel. My daddy could do no wrong in my eyes even when he allowed me to tag along when he went to visit a woman other than my mother.

When my daddy left, there was no one to protect me like he had done all my life. That is when things those bad things began to happen to me. That is when the love for my daddy turned to hate, and that hate lasted for years.

My daddy seemed to always be in and out of my life. When I was five years old, he left Georgia and didn't come back to see me again until I was ten years old. Even after a five-year separation, the day he returned was the happiest day of my life. It didn't matter that I hadn't seen him in five years. All I wanted to remember that day was I was my daddy's little princess. For short periods I heard from my father at least once every other month. But as time went by, I would only hear from him once or twice a year if I was lucky.

My relationship with my mother wasn't good at all. After my mom and daddy broke up, my mom started going out and drinking all the time, which caused her to be gone a lot, leaving me with my grandmother or aunt. All I could think of was how much I wanted my daddy. I thought if my daddy were there, my life would be so very different.

There was a time when I hadn't heard from my daddy for almost a year. Then on my thirteenth birthday, he sent me a birthday card. I was so mad at him. Almost a year had gone by, and all I got was a birthday card! I asked my mom if I could send the card back to him and her response was, "If that's what you want to do." That's exactly what I wanted to do, and that's exactly what I did. When he got the card back, he called my mother and asked her what size clothing I wore. A few days later he sent me a pair of jeans. I was still mad with him, but I kept the jeans.

In the beginning, my daddy took good care of my mom and me, but after he left, all of that stopped. He could have helped my mom take care of me, but he didn't, which caused me to have to do without a lot of the basic necessities in life.

When I was fifteen years old, I had had enough, so I ran away from home. My mother found me, took me home, and called my daddy to send me to live with him. When she told me what she planned to do, I remember saying, "What for? He doesn't want me."

I knew on the inside that he would have collected welfare for me and tried to get child support from my mother, which would not have been fair because she never tried to collect child support from him.

I soon gave up the idea that I would somehow have a father figure in my life. I began to think that the only way any man would ever love me is if I were willing to sleep with them.

At the age of fifteen, I left home to live with an older man. I contacted my daddy and gave him all my contact information to keep in touch with me. I don't know, maybe I felt that if he knew that his fifteen-year-old princess was living and being intimate with an older man, he would come and rescue me. But that didn't happen. As a matter of fact, I only heard from him once or twice a year. I guess I wasn't worth rescuing.

When my daddy did nothing about me leaving home at such a young age, in my mind, I concluded that the man I left home with would be the man in my life that my daddy wasn't.

Ten years had passed since I had seen my daddy. By this time, I was a grown woman with three children, and my life was a complete mess. I hated my daddy and felt that he was partially to blame for all the bad relationships that I had been involved in.

After God came into my life and saved me, I wrote my daddy a long letter. You would have thought that since Jesus had entered my life, my letter would have been calm, caring, and full of love. But to tell you the truth, I cursed him out all through that letter. This was finally an opportunity for me to release all the anger and hatred that had grown inside of me toward him. Even after we got past the letter, I thought our relationship would be better because we were both proclaiming our salvation.

But nothing changed. The relationship didn't get better. It always seemed as if my daddy always put something or someone else before me. I found myself reliving the failed father-daughter relationship over and over again. I once told my daddy that he should count it as an honor that I called him "daddy" because he didn't deserve to be called daddy. After all, he was never there for me, and he still wasn't there.

I had to allow God to help me because I would have still been that little depressed, angry little girl in a grown woman's body if I didn't. I had to learn how to love my daddy despite what he had failed to do for me and how he treated me. The only way I could really love him was to adopt the love that can only come from God.

So, ladies, I understand what it feels like to want your daddy, and he's never there. Fathers are supposed to be our priest, protectors, and providers. When they are not there to teach their daughter's how a man is supposed to treat them, many girls settle for whatever man comes along. I say to you young ladies that God is a good priest, provider, and protector. God will be there when your daddy is not there. He will put a father figure in your life if you allow him. Please don't reject God when He sends a father figure in your life simply because you still want your daddy. Talk to God and pray for your daddy. Jesus hears you, and He is concerned about you.

CHAPTER 3 - YOU ARE VALUABLE

One day I was riding down the road on my way to the grocery store, and the Lord spoke to me. He said, "If you thought of yourself as valuable, you wouldn't do the things you do." At that time in my life, I thought that I was doing well. I was saved, I had forgiven everyone that had abused and mistreated me, and I had stopped struggling with other issues, so I really thought I was doing well. After the Lord spoke to me, I began doing some of the things that I thought I was delivered from because I wasn't feeling good about myself.

When God sends a warning, we need to take heed. The bible states, "Warning comes before destruction." If I had taken heed to what God was saying, it would have kept me from a whole lot of pain and walking in a lowly place in God. Now that

I look back on it, God was trying to get me to love myself.

If we don't love ourselves, then we can't love others. JESUS commanded us to love our neighbors as ourselves. Now, if you don't love yourself, how can you love someone else? That is impossible because you will always treat people according to the way you feel. I challenge you to learn to love yourself. When you can enjoy being alone with yourself, then other people can enjoy being around you. You must love yourself enough to be by yourself sometimes because there are times when you need peace and quiet. Start seeing yourself the way God sees you. Every morning when you wake up, look in the mirror and tell yourself that you are fearfully and wonderfully made by God. Tell yourself that you are beautiful.

You don't need anyone else to tell you that; tell it to yourself.

I'm trying to help you build your self-esteem because if you continue to walk in low self-esteem, you will always allow people to treat you any kind of way. I want to go back to what God spoke to me because this is how this book came about.

Jesus said in Luke 12:24, "Consider the ravens, for they neither sow nor reap, which have neither storehouse nor barn, and God feeds them. Of how much more value are you than the birds?"

I only want to deal with the last sentence of this verse. Jesus says how much more of value are you than the birds. Let's look at what God did for us. God created us in His image and likeness, and He placed His Spirit in us. He didn't create the birds in

His image and likeness, but He did that for us. If you still do not feel that you are valuable, let's go a little further. God gave His only begotten son for us. He did not have to do it, but HE did. God saw that we needed a savior, so He prepared Himself a body to come in to redeem us back to Himself. That alone should cause us to see ourselves the way that He sees us.

We are the apple of His eye, not the birds, but we are. No matter what you have done or where you have been, the Potter is here to put you back together again. Let Him work on you. Allow God to show you who you are in Him. You are so valuable to Him that Jesus became a sacrifice for you. He didn't have to go to the cross, but He did because He thought about how valuable you are to Him. Thank you, Jesus, for dying for us. Thank you, Jesus, for your Blood covering us.

Jesus saw everything that happened to you, and He is concerned about you. That is why He is allowing me to write this book so that you can understand how precious you are to Him.

Begin to develop a relationship with Jesus, and He will help you in every area of your life.

How do you develop a relationship with Jesus? There are several ways to do this, such as:

> 1) **By spending time in His word**. When you spend time in the word of God, you begin to learn who He is and what He has done for you. Also, you began to learn who you are in Him and what He says concerning you.
>
> 2) **We develop a relationship with Jesus through prayer.** When you love someone or try to build a relationship with them, you begin to spend quality time with them. Start spending time with Jesus. The word of God

says, "If you draw nigh to Him, He will draw nigh to you."

3) **We develop a relationship with Jesus through praise and worship.** When you love someone, you will praise them, and that is the way we should be with Jesus. We should want to praise Him because of who He is, not just because of what He gives us. As you begin to build a relationship with Jesus, you will find out that He is the best thing that can happen to you. When you value something, you protect it, and you cherish it, and that's the same way Jesus is with us. He is our protector and keeper. If we want to be kept, He will keep us.

Learn to value yourself. When I say, "value yourself," I mean, don't let anyone define your worth. I want you to keep this statement in mind throughout this chapter. You are more valuable than you could ever imagine. Cherish who you are despite where you have been or where you are right now. Know that God made you fearfully and wonderfully in Him.

Genesis 1:31 reads, "And God saw everything that He had made and, behold it was very good," therefore we are good because the word of God states that it is so.

Take power back from the devil and walk in the place that God has called you. I want you to know that your past does not determine your future. Please, do not allow your past to keep you out of your future. Even if you have been physically, sexually, and emotionally abused, that does not define who you are. God says that we are the apple of His eye. If God says that, then you are more than what happened to you. You are who HE says that you are.

If you can't say these Affirmation without crying than pray and ask GOD to help you believe this about yourself. Start doing things that make you feel good about yourself. For instance, start doing things that make you happy, start spending time with yourself, learn what you like and what you don't like. For right now start finding what makes you happy without someone telling you what makes you happy.

AFFIRMATION

1. I am healed
2. I am smart
3. I am fearfully and Wonderfully made
4. I am gorgeous
5. I am loving
6. I am whole
7. I have a peace of mind
8. I am honest
9. I am compassionate
10 I love myself

CHAPTER 4 - VALUE YOUR VIRGINITY

As you read this chapter, my prayer is that you will understand that you are more than a booty call or a dumping ground. You are the princesses that God made you be.

I was in a youth meeting one day, and one of the youth leaders made a profound statement. She was talking to teenage and young adult girls, and she said, "Remember that you can become like others who have lost their virginity at any time, but they could never become like you." I felt that it was profound because it is a true statement. You can lose your virginity at any time but put a price tag on it. What I mean by "put a price tag on it" is that you should wait for God to bless you with a husband. I say to you cherish your virginity, don't let anyone pressure you into doing anything that's not right. You don't know what you are getting into when you become sexually active, so please wait for God to send you a husband.

I know other teenagers and young adults are having sex, but does that make it right because they are doing it? No, it doesn't! My motto to my girls is, "You can't miss something that you never had." God cared so much for you that He put laws in place concerning you losing your virginity. Let's look at what God had to say about a girl losing her virginity.

Deuteronomy 22:13-21 reads, "[13] If a man takes a wife and, after sleeping with her, dislikes her [14] and slanders her and gives her a bad name, saying, "I married this woman, but when I approached her, I did not find proof of her virginity," [15] then the young woman's father and mother shall bring to the town elders at the gate proof that she was a virgin. ¹⁶ Her father will say to the elders, "I gave my daughter in marriage to this man, but he dislikes her. ¹⁷ Now he has slandered her and said, 'I did not find your daughter to be a virgin.' But here is the proof of my daughter's virginity." Then her parents shall display the cloth before the elders of the town, ¹⁸ and the elders shall take the man and punish him. ¹⁹ They shall fine him a hundred shekels[b] of silver and give them to the young woman's father because this man has given an Israelite virgin a bad name. She shall continue to be his wife; he must not divorce her as long as he lives. ²⁰ If, however, the charge is true, and no proof of the young woman's virginity can be found, ²¹ she shall be brought to the door of her father's house, and there the men of her town shall stone her to death. She has done an outrageous thing in Israel by being promiscuous while still in her father's house. You must purge the evil from among you."

As can be plainly seen from the scriptures, God is very serious about sex before marriage. In verses 13-19, a man could not speak a lie concerning a woman's virginity. If a man-made an accusation about a woman's virginity to her parents or anyone else, he had to prove that what he was saying was the truth.

The parents wanted to see if the sheets had blood on them, which is the "token of the virgin's virginity." If there wasn't any blood on the sheets, then the men of that city would take the woman in front of her father's house and stone her to death. GOD wanted us to stay pure until He blessed us with a husband.

Teenagers think before you have sex or continue to have sex. I want you to think about you being given to your husband, and your gift to him is the most valuable gift that you could give him, and that is your virginity. Teenagers and young adults think before you give themselves to someone who is not worthy of having them. Look at losing your virginity as being contaminated.

What happens when you become intimate with someone is that a soul tie is formed. What are soul ties? A soul tie is like joining and knitting two people together. There are godly (good) and ungodly (bad) soul ties. Godly soul ties are when God joins or connects you with someone. For example, a marriage, family, and good friends. Ungodly soul ties are when you or the devil cause you to join or connect yourself with someone or something that will bring you harm and pain.

Ladies, stop connecting yourselves to someone or something that God didn't arrange. Seek God before you allow things or people to attach to you. If you stay prayerful, God will show you what to allow in your life and what not to allow in your life.

Parents, do your job and stay prayerful so that God will show you when your child or children are getting into the wrong things. I remember when my oldest daughter was 15 years old, and she was friends with this girl that I hadn't met. One day she was on the phone talking to her, and I asked her to let me talk to her. I got on the phone and just talked normally to the girl, and when I got through talking to her, I told my daughter to lose her as a friend because that is no one for her to hang with. Just by talking to her, God showed me who she was, so parents, please do your job.

Teenagers and young adults, please listen when someone is trying to tell you the right thing to do. Stop looking at it as someone always trying to tell you what to do and look at it as God loves you so much that He wants what's best for you. Isaiah 55:8-9 states, "For my thoughts are not your thoughts, neither are your ways my ways," declares the Lord.[9] "As the heavens are higher than the earth, so are my ways higher than your ways and my thoughts than your thoughts.

God has your destiny in HIS hands. Please follow HIS plans.

CHAPTER 5 - THE HEALING

I want you all to know that when you forgive, then you can heal inside. I had gone through most of my life, virtually for years, with low self-esteem, un-forgiveness, bitterness, and rejection reigning on the inside of me. I used to have nightmares of a man raping my oldest daughter, and the thought of that dream used to tear me apart inside. I couldn't sleep at night because I didn't want to have that dream. I became so protective of my children that I wouldn't let them spend the night with any of their friends.

They weren't even allowed to go outdoors by themselves. I didn't want what happened to me to happen to them. I started to have many issues with my oldest son, so I had to get him a counselor. One day the counselor came to my house, and I wasn't doing very well. The counselor wanted to know what was wrong with me, and I told her about the dreams that I was having and that I was scared something was going to happen to my children. The counselor told me that the little girl in the dream was me and didn't need to be afraid about something happening to my children. She said that I had to deal with what happened to me to stop living in fear. I was saved and full of un-forgiveness. I was going through so bad, and I said to God, why did you let all this happen to me, you saw all this before it happens to me, and you could have stopped it before it happened to me, but you didn't. I was upset with God because He didn't stop those bad things from happening to me. I said to God, why didn't you stop this? You knew that I would be full of low self-esteem, un-forgiveness, anger, bitterness, and rejection. God didn't speak to me right away because I was blaming Him and having a pity party. When God spoke to me, He ministered to my spirit, not my flesh. God took me to the book of Genesis 3:15 and showed me how the devil knew Jesus was going to come on the scene, and then God took me to the book of Matthew 2. Matthew 2 shows how Herod had all the children two and under killed. The devil was trying to kill Jesus before He could do what He came to earth to do. He said to me, Satan knew that Jesus was going to come on the scene, and Satan did everything to try and stop Jesus before He started His ministry. He said the same with you, Satan knows that I called you, and I placed my Spirit inside you to do a work for me. That's why Satan caused all this pain in your life. God said, "I allowed it because I have work for you to do." He said, "I am going to use what you went through to help many young ladies." After God ministered to me, I started to cry, and I said God help me forgive every one that hurt me.

I made up in my mind to forgive the men that had hurt me. I started to sleep better, but I was still having issues with my mother. I couldn't even sit in the same room with my mom for long because I held everything that I went through against her. I wanted a relationship with my mom, but I hadn't dealt with the anger and unforgiveness that I had towards her.

In 1999 GOD blessed me with my own house, but I was still unhappy because I wanted a relationship with my mom. One evening my friends, my mom, and sisters were at my house. My friends started to pray for all of us, and God spoke to me and said, "Tell your mother that you are sorry for everything you took her through." I got upset with God because I felt like I hadn't done anything to her. I said to God, "She is the one that needs to apologize to me." But I soon humbled myself and apologized to her. I got on my hands and knees and said to her, "Mom, I'm sorry for everything that I did to cause you pain." My mom grabbed me and hugged me so tight. She was crying, and I was crying too. That very moment I felt something break inside of me, and I felt a love for my mom that I had never felt before. God's ways are not like our ways.

Young people, sometimes you must humble yourself for God to heal you inside. I know you feel like your parents should have been there and it would have made your life a lot easier. Well, guess what, they weren't, but God saw, and He covered you, and He kept you through the whole thing. He said, "I see what happen, but I have a plan for your life." He wants to deliver and heal you. Please let God work on you so that you can let go of all the pain. You must stop rehearsing the pain, so you can forgive every one that hurt you. God wants to put the broken pieces back together. He wants to make you all the way whole.

God, I pray for everyone reading this book that has gone through some type of abuse. God, you are the God that heals us. You sent Your word, and You healed us. God, I speak a word of healing over everyone who reads this book. In Jesus mighty name. Jesus helps them let go of all the pain. Help them humble themselves and receive Your healing and deliverance in their lives. I thank You, Jesus, for your healing power touching someone right now, and it is so. In Jesus' name, Amen.

CONTACT THE AUTHOR

To contact the author for book speaking engagements, bulk purchases, or comments, please reach out to:

Nina Johnson

ninajohnson38@gmail.com

(321)960-8265(cell)

Social Media

Facebook: Nina Johnson

www.ingramcontent.com/pod-product-compliance
Lightning Source LLC
Chambersburg PA
CBHW070931270326
41927CB00011B/2817